UNLEASH [YOUR]
HIDDEN WEAPONS
OF MASS PROMOTION

7 Easy to Launch Secrets Designed to Explode Your Income ... Starting Today!

LARRY H. GASSIN

ii

"This book shows you practical, proven methods, techniques, tips and tricks to attract a steady stream of qualified customers – faster, easier and cheaper than ever before."

~Brian Tracy, CEO & President, Brian Tracy International; Author, "Now, Build a Great Business!"; Founder, www.BrianTracy.com

"If you want to learn how to quickly convert your prospects and customers into your own powerful, raving word of mouth marketing machine, then get and apply the simple, proven methods in this book."

~James Malinchak, Featured on ABC's Hit TV Show, "Secret Millionaire"; Founder, www.BigMoneySpeaker.com

Unleash Your Hidden Weapons of Mass Promotion

7 Easy to Launch Secrets Designed to Explode Your Income ….. Starting Today!

Larry H. Gassin

An Imprint of Achievement Books Press

iv

Unleash Your Hidden Weapons of Mass Promotion

7 Easy to Launch Secrets Designed to Explode Your Income ….. Starting Today!

UNLEASH YOUR HIDDEN WEAPONS OF MASS PROMOTION
7 Easy to Launch Secrets Designed to Explode Your Income .....
Starting Today!

Published and printed in the United States of America by
Achievement Books Press

Cover design by Erwin Tito

Gassin, Larry H.
    Unleash your hidden weapons of mass promotion: 7 easy to launch
secrets designed to explode your income....starting today!

ISBN 978-0-692-57122-4

1. Success. 2. Business Growth. 3. Sales. 4. Promotion.
5. Business Relationships. I. Title.

DEDICATION

This book is dedicated to my family, whose examples inspire me, encouragement motivates me and loving support anchors me. Seeing their goodness, capacity and potential causes me to look for those things in others and to create ways to help many breakthrough to reach and achieve their best in business and in life. I am ever grateful and blessed.

ACKNOWLEDGMENTS

Through the years, I have been fortunate to engage with and learn from a number of coaches, mentors and colleagues whose shared ideas, support, lessons and examples have impacted my life and career, each in a different way and at times, unknown to them. While it's not possible to thank everyone and I apologize for any not listed, please know that you are greatly appreciated.

To start, I thank God for the many blessings gifted to me in my life as I have much to be thankful for. Additionally, I express gratitude to Christian Mickelsen, Adam Urbanski, Brian Tracy, James Malinchak, Jack Canfield, Bill Swanson, The members of Toastmasters Club 417, Lynda Bayless, Yousef Shafiee, John Maxwell, Craig Duswalt, Brian Burris, Bruce Whiting, Bob Proctor, Bud and Bunny Barth, Pamela Peak, Jack Nichols, Victor Broski, Rob Swineford, Lisa Gibson, Dan Stern, Ed Griffith, Ed Heyman, Tim Folkers, Glenn Morshower, Jim Napora, Cindy Cowdell, Johnny Smith, John Muir, Kent Parker, Bob Nadal, Ed Kearns, Noah

St. John, Alex Mandossian, Georgina Sweeney, Stephanie Calahan, Alain Azoulay, Brendon Burchard, Rae-Ann Ruszkowski, Lesley Sattin, Alexis Woods, Jill Yamamoto, Judy Lloyd, Rudolph and Dorothy Baldoni, Gretchen Anderson-Helleck, Keaver Brenai, Vic Johnson.

Special thanks to Cat Crews for her help in readying this for publication.

x

TABLE OF CONTENTS

Unleash Your Hidden Weapons of Mass Promotion

7 Easy to Launch Secrets Designed to Explode Your Income ..... Starting Today!

INTRODUCTION

There are two basic business facts that underlie much of what's written here: First, it's never good to waste money and second, we're all continually looking for a consistent and steadily growing stream of new customers and income. In this economy not only do most business owners not have money to waste, in many cases they don't even have enough to spend on the necessities. Notwithstanding that, they're still looking for (no doubt, needing, more than ever) a consistent and steadily growing stream of new customers. But how can they do that without mountains of miracle making money?

In coaching business owners and executives across a wide range of industries and professions for more than 20 years, they've learned through the ups and downs of typical business cycles (although this current one may not feel too typical) that they must identify the resources and assets they have, make do with what they've got, and enjoy the realization that sometimes, less really can be more. That's actually not bad advice to follow in any economy, because it can mean the difference between being able to survive to stay alive or provide a winning edge to produce the golden goose.

Too often, and especially when they find they're facing really tough times, people believe it's what they don't have, or can't do, that holds them back from succeeding. In reality, it's what they don't think they can do that gets in the way or stops them. If it could be sold in 12 ounce containers, I'd say without question that success comes in "cans", not in "cant's".

In looking to the old adage that the best place to hide something is in plain sight, right under somebody's nose, clients have opened their eyes to find some of their best marketing resources – even some of their most powerful assets and tools – were always right there, in plain sight, under their noses. A lot of time, money and effort have been expended by business owners in looking for that "magic bullet" that will blow things wide open for them with the result that too often they end up shooting themselves in the foot.

There are some great resources, tools and solutions "out there", but for jump-starting results more quickly and more powerfully, business owners can take a line from Dorothy in the Wizard of Oz – "there's no place like home." Remember how the scarecrow, tin man, and lion had what they were looking for all along, they just didn't recognize that fact? It's because they didn't know the facts and they were looking beyond the mark. While it is possible for success to be driven by the vision and passion of one person, it is not a journey that one makes by themselves. When it comes to success, one of the simple secrets is that powerful results are built upon powered relationships.

It's time for business owners and professionals of all kinds to open their eyes and uncover those unused, neglected and too often overlooked but incredibly powerful assets. It's time for them to recognize what they already have and can already do – that won't cost them anything. It's time to Unleash Their Hidden Weapons of Mass Promotion to Explode Their Income – Starting Right Now!

Unleash Your Hidden Weapons of Mass Promotion

7 Easy to Launch Secrets Designed to Explode Your Income ….. Starting Today!

"The aim of marketing is to know and understand the customer so well the product or service fits him and sells itself."

~Peter Drucker

Chapter One
Targeted Marketing
Buckshot or bulls-eye?

Welcome to Unleash Your Hidden Weapons of Mass Promotion to Explode Your Income. If you want to build your business more quickly, with more certainty, and for no cost, you're in the right place. Now wherever you are, look at the door that's closest to you. If you're in your car and you're driving while listening to an audio version of this, just picture the door in your office or at home. Just imagine standing about ten yards away from that door and firing a heavy gage shotgun at it - what would happen? Right, you'd blow the door right off the hinges.

Now, what would happen if you placed that door across a football field about 75 yards away and fired that same shotgun? You might not reach that door. And if you did, the scatter wouldn't have much impact. There may be a few pockmarks, but it wouldn't do much. But if you fired a high-powered rifle at that same door about 75 yards away, you could put a hole right through it.

Increasingly businesses are finding that they have been using a shotgun approach to bring down customers in the

4

big game hunt to generate sales. It's very expensive. And it's not working as well as needed. You can spend a lot of money on blind advertising and you don't know who sees it, or if anyone sees it at all. It requires expensive repetition and you really don't know if it will be powerful enough to "pull" in business.

Like the buckshot scatter across the field, it may have little or no impact, even though you've spent the money, time and effort on it. There's an often stated principle in sales that you have probably heard - that it takes seven times the effort to find a new customer as to keep an existing one.

Businesses are finding that spending money, effort and time on existing customers is the opposite of shooting blind. You know exactly who sees it. You can usually get immediate feedback on the impact. And it will help "push" business in the front door. Like the rifle shot, it's focused, precise and powerful.

For our purposes here, I want to show you how to build power relationships that will power up your sales and growth, as well as give you some T.I.P.S. - Tools, Insights, Principles and Strategies - that will help you convert your customers into a raving massive word of mouth sales machine. On top of that, help you get them to eagerly buy more from you and energetically refer more business to you.

I'm not saying there's no place for advertising. But I do want to give you some useful and meaty tools that you can use and start applying today to help you think differently about your customers, your business and your success. Because when you come down to it, we're all really looking for more and better consistently dependable results to grow our businesses.

There are those who are perpetually looking for the magic bullet to solve their problems and they never find it. Usually, they end up completely losing sight of their target and shoot themselves in the foot. There are a lot of so-called experts out there that will throw complicated and expensive tactics at you that most people either can't figure out how to use or they're just too costly.

In more than twenty years of coaching clients across a broad range of industries to achieve successful results, together we found that the best results generally come from basic, simple and uncomplicated, time tested, tried and true principles that are consistently applied in the framework of clearly defined goals and purposes.

I liken it to the story of the little ten-year-old boy who was riding his bike and came upon a scene that fascinated him. Apparently, there was a large freight truck that entered a tunnel and was about two inches too tall to make it through and got stuck, or wedged in. It couldn't move forward or backward.

The fire department was there with a big hook and ladder truck, which is what got his attention. There was a whole crew of people, engineers and experts trying to use crowbars and jackhammers to help. The jaws of life were even being used to try and cut part of the top off the truck's cab, but all without any luck.

Absolutely fascinated, watching and sizing things up, the little boy finally approached one of the fireman and tugging on his jacket asked, "Hey, why don't you just let some air out of the tires?" You know, that was a much simpler and less costly solution and one that would get faster results.

That's going to be the approach that we take here. In any economy, it's never wise to needlessly expend funds or effort. And it's absolutely foolish to do something well that shouldn't be done at all. But in your personal economic situation, it's even more critical to be smart with your assets. Yet, businesses still need to grow and survive and thrive. So I'm going to share 7 Easy to Launch Secrets that are absolutely free, or cost practically nothing, that will help you explode your income quickly.

CAUTION: Don't be fooled or misled because these secrets may seem simple or even obvious after we expose them, or because it seems "too easy." There's real power in each one and if you're not employing them, you're absolutely leaving money (and probably clients) "on the table."

As an extra bonus, I'm first going to let you know how NOT to set the stage to grow your business and referrals - or the top three minefields that everyone walks into - and how to avoid them so you don't ensure that your business will blow up.

"A man must be big enough to admit his mistakes, smart enough to profit from them, and strong enough to correct them."

~John C. Maxwell

Chapter Two
Avoiding Some Common Mine Fields
Mind-messing maddeningly misguided marketing mistakes

So let's get started. First, the bonus tips on how NOT to set the stage to ask for more business and referrals. The first way is to not promise personal attention or to promise a personal touch and not deliver. In fact, you don't want to promise anything and not deliver in business. What you end up doing is setting the prospect's or customer's expectation high and then force-feeding them disappointment because you're cutting corners to try and somehow make the commitment or simply "appear" to make the commitment you've made.

I have a great example of this. A friend of mine said he'd gone to his dentist and the dentist was bragging to him how he'd gone to a seminar about building dental practices and marketing. The seminar speaker said it would be great to send a personal birthday card to his patients - that it would be a really good personal touch.

Well, my friend forgot about that. And a couple of months later, he came home, got the mail and saw something from the dentist. Then he remembered the conversation and was excited to see what the old doc had sent.

When he opened it up to get this personal touch birthday card, he saw that it had been signed using a rubber stamp. Can you imagine that? What message would be conveyed? I know what my friend thought because I asked him. He said, "I bet the dentist never even saw it. He doesn't even know it's my birthday. He has his secretary do this for everybody. And I'm not special at all!"

If you think about that situation and put yourself in my friend's spot, when that dentist says that your referrals will get the same personal attention you get and asks you for referrals, how fast would you be likely to refer people to that dentist? NOT! You really don't want to ever do something like that when you promise something personal.

A lot of businesses today are promising a personal touch, hand holding, closer coordination and attention. But they don't deliver. It's typical to say what they need to get the sale. And after that, customers are on their own. Do you do that? That's one of the quickest ways to lose clients.

Especially today in such a competitive market when there are wolves at the door of your clients trying to take them. A second minefield to avoid is the scenario of showing up for meetings the wrong way. How do you show up? When do you show up? Do you show up late? Or do you show up early? And what are you about when you get there? Most people show up trying to make a sale.

You know how it is because we've all been through that. If someone's trying to make a sale, you can smell it a mile away. You can just feel it and sense it and your guard goes up. Your defenses are up and registering and you just don't want to have anything to do with it.

That makes a big difference. Whether you're on the phone or whether you're connecting face-to-face with customers or prospects, your attitude transcends every bit of your communication and impacts the level of trust that they have or could have with you.

Years ago, when my children would need to go somewhere, I would often times offer and volunteer. Usually I'd have to race home from work to do it or come from a meeting and it just seemed that I was always cutting it too close for comfort for them.

One time I offered to take them somewhere and they said, "No. That's okay. We'll have mom do it." When I asked them why they said, "We can't trust you." I was pretty surprised. But I shouldn't have been. I'd never gotten them anywhere late but they just didn't like the drama of having to "rush" and deal with being seen as "irresponsible."

One time when my youngest son was ten, he couldn't take it anymore. He got fed up with the stress that he would experience waiting for me to show up on time. So he poked me in the chest and said, "Dad, let me tell you how it is, all right? When you're supposed to be somewhere and you arrange to meet somebody, it's like you promised to meet them there at a certain time. It's like a promise, Dad. So when you're going to go somewhere, to actually get there early is on time. If you arrive on time, that's actually late. And to be late is absolutely, positively unacceptable! Do you get it, dad?" Wow! I said, "Yes, I got it." Right in the heart. Wisdom from a ten-year-old.

Lesson learned and improvements made. But you want to be wary of showing up late because that shows disrespect for the prospect or the customer. It also shows disrespect for you. It really does. It shows that you don't value your word and that you don't value your commitment and your time. If you don't value your commitment and your word on the front end, how can they think you're going to value any commitments made in that meeting or subsequently when you're trying to build up relationships with them? Showing up to make a customer builds a relationship and a potential long-term revenue and referral stream while showing up to make a sale may be a shortsighted one-time "fix." How do you show up?

The third minefield to avoid is, well, rather than trying to explain it, telling you a story as an example would be the best way to share it with you. A friend of mine was a mechanic who turned financial planner. Someone had come into his shop one day and told him that he could make a lot of money as a financial planner, selling investment instruments, retirement investments, insurance and things like that.

So he went through the training and became a financial planner. One day he called me up and asked if I'd meet with him. I was curious and wanted to see what he did. The coach in me wanted to see how he did it and see if there was anything I might do to help him because he was a friend.

We spent a couple of hours together. All he did was tell me the products he could sell, the commissions he could make, what the company wanted him to do, and how the program was going to work for him. Then he asked me this question, which just astonished me. He said, "Hey, now that I've helped you, will you give me three referrals?"

I thought. "HELP me? Help ME? You've just given me four reasons - your presentation and the three referrals you asked for - not to refer anybody to you." He didn't understand some basic principles in doing business including that people are more likely to do business with you if they know you, like you and trust you.

Could you have any confidence in this guy? I knew him and he's a great guy. But absolutely not. There's no way that I would be eager to refer him to somebody and put them through the same thing that I had just gone through. He didn't understand one highly critical lesson in business these days. It's that although people who hardly know you may casually take you home with them without thinking twice, don't you dare expect even your best friends to casually invite you into their Rolodex. They'll protect their referral network with more ferocity than they'll protect their virtue. Referrals have become the prize currency of exchange in business building and people want to keep theirs in "mint" condition.

You've probably heard of people that have made a fortune "overnight" as internet marketers when they get access to someone else's Rolodex, or the list that others have spent a lot of time, money and years building up. There are people that have made overnight fortunes on the Internet exactly by having such access. They must have a strong relationship and be trustworthy to take care of that sacred Rolodex trust. Because that's your future and your livelihood. If you think about your client list and your prospects, you're not going to just give that away willy nilly to people. That's your future. You'll give away something else, but not that. To do so, or to expect other people to do so for you, is a big mistake because it shows that you're not someone that they're going to be a strategic partner with. These days, nobody's rolling out their Rolodex that easily.

Those are three things to avoid: (1) Promising the personal touch and not delivering; (2) Showing up late for meetings or showing up looking for a sale instead of looking to make a customer. If you think about it, one is a long-term income generating solution. The other one's a one-time, short-term fix; (3) trying to take advantage and abuse the idea of someone's Rolodex.

So how DO you set the stage to get more business and referrals? What are the 7 Secret Weapons to Launch? Let's find out.

"The man who does more than he is paid for will soon be paid for more than he does."

~ Napoleon Hill

Chapter Three
Secret Weapon #1
Killer Service and Value
The great equalizers

One of the first things that we must do to get more business is realize that everything is becoming so globalized and computerized that it's becoming commoditized. People can sit home in their pajamas and shop on the Internet, whether it's for personal items and goods or for business items and services. They can sit at their desk at work. They shop and a lot of people have come to adopt the attitude that all you have to do is find the lowest price. The presumption being everything's basically the same.

Two of the biggest ways to stand out and take the focus off price are to (1) deliver a killer service. Just absolutely killer service. And the other is (2) to deliver more value than people pay for. Let me give you an example of each.

A simple example of killer service would be if you've gone to a nice restaurant and the waiter or waitress is near your table, keeping an eye on your party if you're with a big group. And although they are not part of your group, they're very aware of what you're doing and what your needs are.

They see when someone's water needs to be refilled, when someone needs some more wine. If a napkin or a piece of silverware drops, they come over and they're right there on the spot with it. They help make it a wonderful experience and it's seamless. And you don't have to ask anything. You don't have any unmet needs because your needs are anticipated and addressed. Your needs are taken care of. All you have to do is be there and enjoy the experience.

Now, as far as delivering more value than people pay for, I think a great example is, again going to the restaurant, the Claim Jumper restaurants. I've never heard anyone assert that the Claim Jumper is the "finest" restaurant in town. But they do work very hard to give you a great meal and huge portions. You can go to Claim Jumper and usually take half a meal home and eat it the next day. They give you a lot of value, perceived value, for the money.

So those are two ways to take the focus off of price commoditization. When you do this effectively (and genuinely), you can focus on relationships, service and quality – areas where you can stand out and shine in unique and incomparable ways and make it impossible for others to compete.

Action Guide – Secret Weapon #1

What are some ways it would significantly impact your business if you were to start delivering truly killer service and over-deliver on value?

1. _____

   _____

   _____

2. _____

   _____

   _____

3. _____

   _____

   _____

What will be the cost to your business – lost opportunities, lost revenue, lost clients, lost reputation - and to you - if you don't, and keep things just as they are now?

_____

_____

_____

_____

Which specific clients/customers do you need to focus this attention on immediately?

_____

_____

_____

What are 3 actions you can quickly take (they don't need to be "huge", they just need to be genuine and sustained – and started) to deliver killer service and incredible value?

1. _____

   _____

   _____

2. _____

   _____

   _____

3. _____

   _____

   _____

Great, now what date will you start each of these?

1. _____

2. _____

3. _____

"Trust is the glue of life. It's the most essential ingredient in effective communication. It's the foundational principle that holds all relationships."

~Stephen Covey

Chapter Four
Secret Weapon #2
Give People a Reason to Buy and Refer Like Crazy
Facilitating the friendship factor and forgetting fear

The second thing you want to do is give people a reason to buy more and refer more business to you. As I said before, we've all heard the adage that people will do business with you if they know you, like you and trust you.

But I want to add one more characteristic that makes a huge difference. I've found that it causes the response to go up perhaps ten times. Restated, it's that besides knowing you, liking you and trusting you, ***they know that you know them***. When they know that you know them, their trust goes up dramatically. And so does their resistance to change to someone else.

Why would they leave to deal with someone that doesn't know them? A competitor has no idea what the customer or prospect are about, what they need, or what they want. Again, that allows you to focus on quality, service and relationships and that's where you can control the game.

There's another huge benefit of building business relationships by building this in. When they know you know them and about them – their business, their family, their likes, dislikes, etc. – and you've shown interest by using the secret weapons in this book, you are elevated beyond being merely a service provider/vendor to being someone with whom they feel they have a personal relationship and finally to being a friend.

Here's the great part. If you make a mistake they're more inclined to just let you make it right – make up any losses or costs incurred (of course, as a friend you'd want to do that, right!) rather than go for punitive damages and replace you with someone else. They wouldn't do that to a friend. You can even use such crises as opportunities to further strengthen that relationship and reinforce it with your client. Think of ways you can get to know them – and show it – to your clients. I'll also discuss more about this later.

(Action Guide Starts Next Page)

Action Guide – Secret Weapon #2

What are some ways it would significantly impact your business if you were to focus on "knowing your clients/customers" and making sure they knew you know?

1. _____

_____

_____

2. _____

_____

_____

3. _____

_____

_____

What will be the cost to your business – lost opportunities, lost revenue, lost clients, lost reputation - and to you - if you don't, and keep things just as they are now?

_____

_____

_____

_____

Which specific clients/customers do you need to focus this attention on immediately?

_____

_____

_____

What are 3 actions you can quickly take (they don't need to be "huge", they just need to be genuine and sustained – and started) to let your customers know, like and trust you better, and recognize and value that you know them?

1. _____

_____

_____

2. _____

_____

_____

3. _____

_____

_____

Great, now what date will you start each of these?

1. _____

2. _____

3. _____

"Personal relationships are the fertile soil from which all advancement, all success, all achievement in real life grows."

~Ben Stein

Chapter Five
Secret Weapon #3
Connecting

The people-pleasin' power of purely personal

Another way to have more favorable impact upon
your prospects and customers is to connect with them. I
mean, really connect. I talked about the dentist before
who was going to send out the personalized birthday cards
with the rubber stamp from the secretary. But you can
actually send out a hand signed birthday card. Or you can
make a quick call to people on their birthday. I have made
thousands of calls to clients, friends and prospects on their
birthdays. When I hear it's someone's birthday, if it's
someone I think that I'm going to be contacting or
communicating with again in the future, I'll generally
make a note of it. You can do it as simply as this: You
can call up in a minute to a minute and a half, you can
have an impact on them and be sincere. And they can feel
it.

Here's an example. If Joe's my client and it's his birthday,
I call him up. He answers the phone. I say, "Hey Joe - it's
Larry. How are you doing?" "Just fine." And I say, "I
just wanted to wish you a happy birthday. I know it's your

birthday. I was thinking about you and wanted to let you know you were on my mind. And I really appreciate our friendship. Our business relationship for sure, but I also appreciate the personal level of the relationship that we've developed.

"And I just want to wish you a happy birthday and see what are you and Deb going to do tonight? Are you going to go out and paint the town? Or are you going to have a quiet night at home? Any idea of what you're going to do? And he'll tell me and I'll say, "That's great."

"Well, listen. I don't want to take up a lot of your time. I know you're busy there. But I did just want to let you know I was thinking about you and wish you a happy birthday. Say hi to Debbie. You guys have a good time tonight, all right? Talk to you later."

That's it. It's that simple. I've had days where there are nine or ten people important to me whose birthdays are the same day. And in a matter of ten to fifteen minutes I can take care of that and really connect with them. By the way, how many other business professionals do you think call them? Not that many, probably for some of the same reasons you're thinking about hesitating. In a very short time, you can stand out and stand above the crowd of could-be competitors.

There are a couple of things I want to point out. When I asked him "what are you going to do tonight?" I gave him a couple of options. I just left it open. Because it's possible he has no plans. And the last thing I want to do is make him feel awkward because he doesn't have anything going on. I don't want to make him feel inferior, unprepared, or like he has no life. And I also didn't want to back him into a corner. If I only asked him "are you going to go out and celebrate and whoop it up and paint the town?" and if he wasn't and they were going to have a quiet night, I don't want him to feel that I think that's bad.

So I gave both options, opened it up and let him say whatever he's going to tell me and I can tell him it's great. I can share with people that some of my favorite birthdays have been nice quiet evenings if that's what they tell me - because that's the truth. And other times going out and having a good time. And I just say "I'm sure you're going to have a great, awesome time. Have fun."

So you don't want to back them into a corner - because the whole point is to build and strengthen that relationship.

Action Guide – Secret Weapon #3

What are some ways it would significantly impact your business if you were to start being genuinely personal and reach out to clients in order to "reach in" to their hearts?

1. _____

_____

_____

2. _____

_____

_____

3. _____

_____

_____

What will be the cost to your business – lost opportunities, lost revenue, lost clients, lost reputation - and to you - if you don't, and keep things just as they are now?

_____

_____

_____

_____

Which specific clients/customers do you need to focus this attention on immediately?

_____

_____

_____

What are 3 actions you can quickly take (they don't need to be "huge", they just need to be genuine and sustained – and started) to really connect in new ways that make your relationships with clients more personal to them?

1. _____

_____

_____

2. _____

_____

_____

3. _____

_____

_____

Great, now what date will you start each of these?

1. _____

2. _____

3. _____

"Each of us finds his unique vehicle for sharing with others his bit of wisdom."

~Ram Dass

Chapter Six
Secret Weapon #4
Show Them You're Thinking About Them
When you remember people, they remember you

Another way to connect with people is to send them news articles or stories about their interests. When you get to know people, and this shows you know them, you can send them news clippings and articles. If you see something, just take a pen ... usually a blue pen's good because it stands out from the newsprint or the print in magazines. And just let them know, "Hey Joe - Saw this article that dealt with what we were talking about (or where you're trying to take the company.) and I thought it might be interesting to you. Hope it's helpful." And just sign your name.

I'd recommend that you even designate a set time each day or each week to scan magazines, newspapers, the Internet, whatever you're looking at for opportunities to connect with your clients. And if you have some significant clients in certain industries or areas, you might want to subscribe to something online or in print that would give you additional insight into what's going on in their industry. While it's not a crystal ball, it may be the next best thing. It will surely put you in a league of your own; distinctly on top of any would be competitors who want your clients. Most importantly, it will re-affirm that you KNOW them and that they are important to you. Then their trust in you can increase and the value of your relationship will become more important to them. Just think of it as a power path for promoting prosperity – theirs and yours.

Bottom line: it lets them know that you're thinking about them. Not only are you sending them *something*, you're sending them articles and items that might be helpful and that pertain to what they're doing and where they're at. So that's a great way to connect personally and help increase both of your bottom lines.

(Action Guide Starts Next Page)

Action Guide – Secret Weapon #4

What are some ways it would significantly impact your business if you were to set aside a little time to think about your clients - their needs and goals – and offer help or suggestions like articles, industry tips, notes of encouragement or interest, etc., to let them know they matter even when they're not with you?

1. _____

_____

_____

2. _____

_____

_____

3. _____

_____

_____

What will be the cost to your business – lost opportunities, lost revenue, lost clients, lost reputation - and to you - if you don't, and keep things just as they are now?

_____

_____

_____

_____

Which specific clients/customers do you need to focus this attention on immediately?

_____

_____

_____

What are 3 actions you can quickly take (they don't need to be "huge", they just need to be genuine and sustained – and started) to provide small moments of high-yield support?

1. _____

_____

_____

2. _____

_____

_____

3. _____

_____

_____

Great, now what date will you start each of these?

1. _____

2. _____

3. _____

"Profit in business comes from repeat customers, customers that boast about your project or service, and that bring friends with them."

~W. Edwards Deming

Chapter Seven
Secret Weapon #5
Can We Talk?

Cashing in with a cornucopia of critical conversations

This next secret weapon has three different explosive devices. Using any one consistently should generate great results. Applying all three should be like adding rocket fuel to your latte – look out! These next three items that I want to go through, the next three tips, I think are some of the best-kept secrets. Launching them will not only help you to find out what your customers want, but why they want it, what they're doing and why they're doing it. They let you know exactly what you need to do or offer to help them – in just the way they need and just when they need it. Translated – just when they're ready to buy. Best of all, it will help prepare them to eagerly refer more business to you.

I call this . . . it's pretty tricky and should have a drum roll . . . I call this "TALK to them!" Talk is cheap…..real cheap……so, "buy" lots of it! I've found so many business owners have problems with clients that would be easily avoided. Partly because they don't talk to their customers. In this age of the digital revolution, people tend to be communicating quickly, casually, copiously, cleverly and CARE-less-ly. They send emails, text messages, instant messages, intentionally leave voice mails, and . . .? (fill in your favorite blank). The one communication clients don't get enough of is to hear your voice - LIVE. They need to have a human interaction.

It's been noted that everyone has access to the same powerful computers, the same programs, the same internet for research and the same marketing and sales tools. What's going to make the strategic difference for success over the next decade or two is the level of real, and real-time, personal service and attention invested in relationships. That's going to be one of the critical factors and high-impact leverage points that will make someone stand out and set them apart from their competitors – real and perceived. That's what your customers and clients are looking for and what they need to help them know that they're in good hands. How can they know if they're in good hands if they don't even know whose hands they are in and they've not met with you for some time? This goes back to what I discussed earlier: beyond doing business with people they know, like and trust, customers may be 10 times more likely to especially do business with those that have shown they also know the customer.

One of the main themes in Tom Peters' and Robert Waterman's book, **"In Search of Excellence,"** is: "Excellent companies are better listeners. They benefit from market closeness. *Most of their innovation comes from the market. From listening. From inviting customers into the company and paying attention to what they want.*" (Italics added.)

 I recommend you read that quote again. There is great insight and a powerful key to accelerating your success contained in it, so be sure to let it "distill" upon your mind. I find that too many companies - in their websites, marketing materials, promotional pieces and "can't get off the ground floor" elevator pitches - want to be understood, rather than show they understand. They want to show how "good" they are rather than how they can help prospects and clients become better. They work to show the prospects and clients what they can get from "my menu of items for sale" rather than demonstrating that they "get the client" better than anyone else understands them and can help them solve the exact problems they need help with.

So let me share with you several simple ways you can do that. One is when you talk to them, ask them what problems they're having as you "explore" while you spend time with them. Identify what problems they're having that you might either be able to help them solve yourself or that you might be able to refer them to someone that you know that could do a great job to help them solve the problem.

Research has shown that if you can be a great referral source, a "go to" person for a client five to seven times, you will develop front of mind presence. And wouldn't it be great if every time they had a problem and they needed something solved, they thought, "Hey, I'll just call YOU. You've always got someone great. You've got a great set of resources. You've got access to all kinds of people. And you know how to get the job done. You've never steered me wrong." If you do that, you become permanently valuable to your customers, and potentially, to their network.

Let me give you a quick example. A CPA that I was coaching is a great guy and a terrific human being who is very talented and has good business insights. I asked him why he thought his clients deal with him. He had never asked himself that question as he was just too busy trying to get, hoping to get, clients.

So when I pushed him a little bit, he said, "Well, I suppose good service for a fair price." I just knew that wasn't the answer. That just would not be why people would go to him. They might value that from him. But that wouldn't be what most attracts them as clients.

When you want to build your business, you need to know what grabs and attracts prospects to you and what holds your customers in the first place -- why people do business with you. When you find out what those hot buttons are, or what your natural gifts are, you can use that knowledge to your advantage. It's also to your prospective customers' advantage. Because that's the help they need.

So this CPA's assignment was to survey thirty of his clients by either going to lunch with them, calling them on the phone, or stopping by and visiting them. If you think about it, just taking those actions would make him stand out, right? So he asked and it was the most interesting thing to him. Out of the thirty people that he interviewed, only two even mentioned fair fees, fair rates, good pricing, good service, etc. Most didn't even mention it. It wasn't their top concern.

He got answers like "I totally trust you." "I sleep well at night knowing you're taking care of me." One of his clients said, "you're the first CPA that my wife has liked and that we're comfortable going to and having all of our financial matters revealed to you." "We know you've got a good feeling for what's going on with our family and our needs. And you anticipate our needs better than we do." "You just have a great business head on you. You have a great sense for business and you help us grow our business." Hardly anything (except two instances) was mentioned about price or good service.

So what it told him and what he learned is there's a whole lot about him that's communicated to his clients that he didn't even take advantage of. And it's a good chance, 99 percent sure, that if you push those particular hot buttons consistently for a broad number of people that you're going to be pushing those same hot buttons with other people you interact with. You'll want to adjust your marketing materials, your marketing approach and your presentations to include opportunities to push these same hot buttons for those you meet, because that will get you more business – more easily.

Another way to do it is to approach your customer, let's say his name is Joe and say something to the effect of, "Hey Joe, as one of my most important customers, what are some things I could do for you that would be so different, unusual or so overwhelming that you'd actually feel compelled to tell your colleagues and associates about me? I really want to know so I can do an even better job for you."

Now, what this tells (Joe) your clients is ... that they matter, that their opinion matters, their referrals matter and that you're looking for more business. Too often, especially with professional service providers, business owners want to impress their clients that they're busy so they think they've got a good practice going. But that then tells them that they shouldn't give referrals, as they may not have room for more customers.

So this approach lets them know you are looking for business. And it also lets them know that you just don't expect it and take it for granted, that you want to do more than "earn it", as so many people say. You want to actually treat them so outstandingly and provide service that's so overwhelming that they feel a need to refer others to you so that they can receive the same thing.

There are several things about this you need to be aware of and keep in mind. You don't ever want to ask your customer "what's **one thing** or what are **one or two things** I could do for you that would be so different, unusual and overwhelming that you feel compelled to tell your colleagues and associates about me?"

If you narrow it down to one or two and he gives you one or two things, it's possible you either can't, or don't do those things. It could be because of your capacity or the cost to do it. It could be a result of a difference in values. It may be something you just don't do.

Plus, regardless of the reason, if it's something that doesn't get done, your customer is left thinking, "you asked me what I wanted, what I needed, what would do the job. I told you and you didn't do that."

So you want to ask them for **some** things. "What are some things I can do for you . . . ?" Because if they give you one or two, say, "I appreciate that. What are a couple more? Are there anymore?" Get four, five, or six things. That way when you do one, two or three of them, they'll know you were listening. And you'll have an option to do those that you can attain and those that you're comfortable doing. Then they know that you're paying attention, that you're listening - and that they matter and their opinion matters.

The third explosive device along these lines would be to give your customers an opportunity to be heroes to their clients, their associates, their contacts, and to their Rolodex. Let me tell you a story that demonstrates this.

Sue was a registered physical therapist. She was extremely outstanding and skilled in the technical aspects of her profession and also has what I call incredible bedside marketing manner. She had an out of state patient who had never had that kind of help and treatment from anyone. It was such an impressively packaged deal of great physical care and great bedside marketing care, that he's made it his personal mission to give Sue at least one referral a month from her local area. He knows out of state people would not be good for her. And he does that - gives her at least one referral a month, more when he can. And the reason he does that is he's looking for opportunities to be a hero to his contacts and expose them to Sue. Okay, are you with me?

Now ask yourself this question: "What can I do differently that would make it easy for my customers to be heroes by referring their network to me for my services or products?" Now we're starting to get into some good things.

If you're going to have someone do business with you, you don't want to make it hard for them to reach you or to let you know what they need in order to do business with you. A lot of businesses actually make it hard for customers to get in the door and do business with them. But what could you do differently? What could you do more of or what should you do less of that would be different and make it easy for your customers to be heroes by referring their network to you for your services or products?

For an example, let me go back to the restaurant. I'm sure this has happened to most of us. Have you ever gone to a new restaurant, it's your first time there, and the food, the service or the atmosphere were so unbelievably outstanding or everything was just perfect? It doesn't have to be fancy or expensive. It could be a place where it's just too much fun.

When you've gone to a place like that and everything was so unbelievably outstanding, didn't you immediately think of when you could come back and who you could bring with you? Why'd you do that? Right - you wanted to be a hero. You wanted to stand out for a great find, something of huge value, something that is new and different. Something that is beyond the norm of what your contacts or friends or colleagues would be experiencing. You wanted the chance to be a hero.

You need to do things that would give your customers and clients a chance to be a hero with their network and their contacts and cause them to have a desire, their own desire ... you're not even asking them ... that they want to refer business to you. And they want to let people experience the same thing that they're experiencing with you.

Wow, would that be awesome? It's do-able. I want you to know it is do-able because I have clients that have done that. I've heard of some advertising research that showed that one customer well taken care of could be more valuable than $10,000 worth of advertising. So far, the things that we've gone over are essentially free.

The most expensive thing would be a birthday card. I actually have a service I use that's automated and has scanned my handwriting into it. I can change the font color to stand out even more. It's my personal, recognizable signature that goes out on a card. And I can just send them from my desk and put my own personal messages in them. It's warm, still looks and feels personal and clients have loved it.

A noteworthy distinction is that a satisfied customer is just that – satisfied. Customers expect to be at least "satisfied" and therefore have no reason to go out of their way for you. They've received what they paid for. Think back to Secret Weapon #1 – Killer Value.

Understand, the customers you give that outstanding service to, or wow them, will get you more sales and more customers. If you take fantastic care of your customers, they will gladly open doors for you that you could never open by yourself.

You want to be so good at this that the only question that your clients ask is, "Why would I ever deal with someone who was second best to you?"

(Action Guide Starts Next Page)

Action Guide – Secret Weapon #5

What are some ways it would significantly impact your business if you were to offer your clients a real-time live and interested voice, who knew what their needs and hot-buttons are, overwhelmingly "wow" them and become a "hero experience" they feel they "must" share with others, and make potential competitors irrelevant?

1. _____
   _____
   _____

2. _____
   _____
   _____

3. _____
   _____
   _____

What will be the cost to your business – lost opportunities, lost revenue, lost clients, lost reputation - and to you - if you don't, and keep things just as they are now?

_____

_____

_____

_____

Which specific clients/customers do you need to focus this attention on immediately?

_____

_____

_____

What are 3 actions you can quickly take (they don't need to be "huge", they just need to be genuine and sustained – and started) to identify client needs/wants and win and wow them over?

1. _____

_____

_____

2. _____

_____

_____

3. _____

_____

_____

Great, now what date will you start each of these?

1. _____

2. _____

3. _____

"We had a branding problem. We have allowed ourselves to be branded by our tragedies. If you said 'Oklahoma City,' chances are the next word out of your mouth was 'bombing.'"

~Mick Cornett

Chapter Eight
Secret Weapon # 6
Building Your Better Brand of You

Money-making moniker management

The next secret weapon that we want to unload is branding. How many businesses do you know that have spent time or money hiring a branding expert to help with their business? There's an old adage in estate tax planning that says if you don't provide your own will, that when you die, the state will provide one for you. But you probably won't like it.

Well, the same thing is absolutely true with regard to your brand – your business name, your reputation, your image and your appeal. If you don't consciously brand yourself or watch what brand you demonstrate you are, others - the marketplace, your customers and prospects, or your competitors - will do it for you. And not only might you not like it, it might cost you plenty. It could cost you lost referrals, which would be a real shame because your business won't grow. But worse, it could cost you lost business from existing customers. Or worst of all, lost customers.

I'm not saying that you should go out and hire a branding consultant, although many people do. What I am suggesting and strongly urging you to do is be aware of the fact that branding is happening everyday and with every customer interaction. You need to plan ahead of time to define and design your proactive responses so you don't have to react and make things worse.

If you're clear on your company's vision, values, mission, goals and the strategies to achieve them - that will form the foundation of any branding you would pay for. They can simply be incorporated into the structured ways you do business and approach customers and their referrals.

You need to ask, "How am I branding myself?" "What brand am I creating?" What brand are you showing that you are by your interaction with people; the way you approach them in meetings; the way you conduct yourself; the way you treat them; the way you treat yourself; how professional you are? You are branding yourself every day in every instance.

Let me share with you a fun example here of brand perception. I have a friend who is a credit card processing merchant. She sells credit card processing services.

That's something that companies commonly get upset about. They don't like the cost or the fees. It can feel complicated to get involved in and setup. They just aren't sure what methods they ought to use or quite how to do it. Often, her prospects will experience "vendor avoidance" when it comes to meeting with people in her field to address these matters because they've heard they're going to be sold over-priced equipment or services they're stuck with for years. It's a great situation in which to ask yourself (as a service provider), "Am I adding to the problems of my prospects and customers, or am I a solution to their problems?"

So I posed the question to her about her brand, "Are you perceived as the diabolically distressing, disputably disinterested, devilish deliverer of discouraging debit and dollar dinging drudgery trying to sell machines to people? Or are you crowned the creatively quintessential, client-concerned, charismatic queen of customer care, quicker cash and credit card ka-ching, ka-ching?"

Are you there selling something to them or are you there to help them with their business so that they'll operate more smoothly, more efficiently and more profitably – and be more loyal to you? Can they see that you're a solution to their problem and not creating more problems? Like a popular credit card commercial asks, "what's in your wallet?" I would strongly suggest you ask yourself "what's in your brand?" What IS your brand?

(Action Guide Starts Next Page)

Action Guide – Secret Weapon #6

What are some ways it would significantly impact your business if you were to identify the brand you're communicating, stop letting others determine that for you, and strategically control the brand you are?

1. _____

_____

_____

2. _____

_____

_____

3. _____

_____

_____

What will be the cost to your business – lost opportunities, lost revenue, lost clients, lost reputation - and to you - if you don't, and keep things just as they are now?

_____

_____

_____

_____

Which specific clients/customers do you need to focus this attention on immediately?

_____

_____

_____

What are 3 actions you can quickly take (they don't need to be "huge", they just need to be genuine and sustained – and started) to either strengthen your brand or strategically rebrand your business to attract, not repel prospects/clients?

1. _____

_____

_____

2. _____

_____

_____

3. _____

_____

_____

Great, now what date will you start each of these?

1. _____

2. _____

3. _____

"Employees are a company's greatest asset - they're your competitive advantage. You want to attract and retain the best; provide them with encouragement, stimulus, and make them feel that they are an integral part of the company's mission."

~Anne M. Mulcahy

Chapter Nine
Secret Weapon #7
Launch Your Most Important Customers
Hunkered down or helping out?

The seventh secret that I want to share with you is the impact of your employees. Your employees are your most important customers. Because they impact - they either impress or distress - all of your paying customers. Please think about that. How do you treat them? Do you treat them well? Do you treat them like they're valuable to you? Do you just treat them like they're time clock punchers and you really don't care about them personally as long as they're not asking to get paid for hours they're not working? Do you treat them as if you don't believe they make much difference, or as if you expect them to contribute and have confidence they will?

I had a great experience with this that taught me a valuable lesson and made a big difference in my business years ago. I had a number of clients who were wealthy members of the community. Several were doctors that were founders of some of the big hospitals in our county. They were on the executive management committees, managing partners, etc. and operated some of the hospitals for part of their tenures.

One in particular was really a good person, but took some pleasure in being a little "crusty" and unsettling people to keep them at bay. He tried to be grumpy, cranky, and crotchety and at times seemed almost angry. One day my receptionist came to me and said, "I just can't take this anymore. Every time he calls, it seems like he's yelling. He snaps and is abrupt with me every time he comes in. It gets me stressed out and I just can't deal with it." I tried sharing with her that's just how he is. That's not how he really feels. And she said she just couldn't take it.

So I said, "Okay. Well, we'll deal with it. Give me about a half hour. Let me think about it. And then come in my office and we'll address it and take care of it." So I thought about it and realized I had a big decision to make. This was one of my biggest clients at the time and I did a lot of work with him. But he was negatively impacting my receptionist. As a result she was not going to give a very favorable interaction or impression to new prospects when they came into the office or to existing clients when they called or came in.

I realized I had to prioritize. She came in and I told her we'd call the doctor and address this with him. So she sat there while I was on the phone. I told him she was in the office. I basically said, "Hey Doc, I've got a problem I need your help on. Can I talk to you for a few minutes?" And he said, "Sure."

I confirmed he knew that he was not only one of my most important clients, but one of my favorites as well. Also that we had a long-standing relationship and that he knew I valued it. I said, "Well, I've got a problem here. You know how you tend to like to bark and snap at people? I just don't pay the receptionist and others here enough to take that - to be yelled at on the phone or intimidated when clients come in the office. Especially by people I like so much. We either have to change something in the approach you take or we're going to have to change something in our relationship."

He understood. In fact, he was really impressed that I would stand up for her and treat her with that much value. We got off the phone and the situation was addressed. My receptionist sat there dumbfounded, with her mouth hanging open. She could not believe I risked one of my biggest clients for her. Her loyalty increased tremendously. She made it her mission to let people know that I was the best guy and this was the only office they should ever go to. And no one was going to give them the kind of caring and attention and service that I would give them. And she became a great raving word of mouth employee. It was wonderful.

The funny thing was the next time the doctor came in the office, she said, "Hi doc. You know, I'm sorry about that. I didn't mean anything." And he said, "Oh, that's okay. I know." She said, "You know, you're really a nice guy." He just smiled at her, got this big grin and snapped, "Don't you dare tell anybody!" They had an even better relationship after that.

There's another story that talks about the importance of taking care of your employees, how you treat them and how you empower them that occurred with Southwest Airlines. As you may know, Southwest Airlines likes to be a little humorous and their ads are a little bit different. They're lighthearted and like to enjoy their passengers and customers so that they enjoy flying on the airline. As one of the flight attendants was going through the routine of all the safety instructions, she made a couple of jokes.

There was a lady on the flight that thought that wasn't very funny.

This lady sent a letter complaining to Herb Kelleher, the President of Southwest Airlines. She said that she thought that light-hearted attitude was totally uncalled for and wanted to know what he was going to do about it. He wrote back a simple two-line letter that said, "Thank you for your note. We're sure going to miss you on Southwest Airlines." He did not want to negatively impact his employees. Everyone (well, almost everyone) liked Southwest's humorous approach, and it worked. It was important to them as a company, as a culture and as a brand, that they were lighthearted, fun and creative. They were the fun, enjoyable, "move around the country" airlines to travel on. He was willing to lose a customer to support and send an important message to his employees.

How do you treat your employees? They're the ones that take care of *YOUR* customers. Your employees will unconsciously communicate volumes to your clients of whether you want the clients to come back, whether you value your clients and whether you keep your promises - implied and explicit. It's critical because they communicate all that without even knowing it.

I had another experience several years ago. One of my daughters and her children were visiting. They flew out on Midwest Airlines. I literally had never even heard of Midwest Airlines. On their return home, I took them to Los Angeles International airport where their plane was supposed to leave at 2:30 pm. I had received approval ahead of time to accompany her through security to the gate because she had two small children, a stroller, car seats, diaper bag, her purse and carry-on bag. That was a lot for one person to deal with.

About two minutes after she boarded the plane, everybody rushed back out of the plane. There was a light on somewhere in the plane. They worked on fixing it for an hour and a half or two and then announced they thought it would be another hour or two until they could find the problem and fix it.

Midwest then told all the passengers in their area that they would give them a voucher for a free meal in the airport while they were waiting, which seemed very nice. A little while later they re-boarded the plane and then found that they still couldn't fix the problem. It was actually a problem with the steering mechanism - which I think is a good thing to find out before you take off. Apparently, the only way to fix it was to fly out one of their mechanics from Kansas that had a special tool because for some reason, they didn't have it at LA. It was only about a five minute job to fix, but they needed the right tool. So they brought in a plane at 9:30 pm that night. They cleaned it, refueled it, put the people on it and let them take off late at night.

I was thinking it was a good thing I had been waiting there in the airport with her, as it was more than 7 hours. As I was leaving, I happened to be walking out with the gate supervisor of Midwest Airlines and a customer who'd flown Midwest before. We talked about the situation that day and the impact on the customers and the airline employees, who all had stayed overtime until this was resolved.

The other guest started raving wildly about Midwest Airlines, saying how it was the greatest airline in the world and that she flew it whenever she could. She explained Midwest was the last airline to use white linen and crystal glasses aboard their flights and that without any question, it was just a super airline. Then I noticed the supervisor took great pride. She was very genuinely apologetic and started boasting about all the things, in a good way, that Midwest does for their passengers and for their guests.

I was very impressed by this. Then, saying how she recognized I had been there all day, she offered me a voucher for a flight on Midwest Airlines so I could experience it. She also offered to have me reimbursed for my parking since I had been there all day long.

Did I say I was impressed? I'd never heard of Midwest Airlines before that day but I was their newest raving fan. I started asking everybody I knew that traveled and was in business, both clients and friends, if they were flying Midwest. If they said, "No," I'd ask them, "Why not?" I would briefly share my experience and say that's the airline to fly.

After that, I flew Midwest a few times and it was a great airline. It was comfortable and very nice. But it was that customer service, the way they treated their employees and the authority they gave them that empowers them to really take care of business – and more particularly to really take care of their customers - that converted me to be a raving fan. And I was in fact a raving word of mouth maniac for them. Do you see? They made it easy for me to be a hero and open up my network to them.

76

Action Guide – Secret Weapon #7

What are some ways it would significantly impact your business if you were to start genuinely viewing and treating your employees and associates as if they were your most important clients/customers, let them deepen their loyalty and help them create business-building opportunities for you?

1. _____

   _____

   _____

2. _____

   _____

   _____

3. _____

   _____

   _____

What will be the cost to your business – lost opportunities, lost revenue, lost clients, lost reputation - and to you - if you don't, and keep things just as they are now?

_____

_____

_____

_____

Which specific employees/associates do you need to focus this attention on immediately?

_____

_____

_____

What are 3 actions you can quickly take (they don't need to be "huge", they just need to be genuine and sustained – and started) to ensure your most important assets do not depreciate and to confirm and clarify their value to them?

1. _____

   _____

   _____

2. _____

   _____

   _____

3. _____

   _____

   _____

Great, now what date will you start each of these?

1. _____

2. _____

3. _____

"You can't control the marketplace. But you can absolutely control your place in the market."

~Larry Gassin

Chapter Ten
Your Secret Weapons Shouldn't Be Secret
Conclusion
The most absurd hiding place of all

I'd like to finish up by asking you a couple of questions. Would you benefit by sharpening up your marksmanship and start using a high-powered rifle instead of a shotgun to get your sales and customers? If things aren't the way you want them to be with regard to your sales and business growth; if you're losing money or you're leaving too much on the table; are you going to keep doing what you've been doing? Won't that just ensure that you're going to keep getting what you've been getting? Or will you take decisive action to really evaluate what you've been doing, even getting coaching or other help if needed, to create a roadmap and an action plan for massively improved success?

In the economy you're in, you certainly know that it has been a very difficult market for many people, perhaps for you, and for many of your customers and clients. *You can't control the marketplace. But you can absolutely control your place in the market.*

There's a story called "Acres of Diamonds" which you may be familiar with. It's about a man who owned some land and wanted to go out and search the world for wealth. Because he wanted to acquire wealth he spent his life searching for this - but never found it. When he died, his land was sold to somebody else who started tilling it, smoothing it out, leveling it, and just trying to improve the land a little bit.

One day as they were digging, they found diamonds. There were literally acres of diamonds on this man's land and he died not knowing it. You see, each of us have some acres of diamonds right where we stand, right where we are. You have gifts and talents. You have abilities. But beyond that, you have customers. You have employees. And you have the opportunity to watch the value of your business grow so you can mine those acres of diamonds at no cost or extremely low cost just by taking care of them.

Don't let your hidden weapons of mass promotion stay buried right under your nose. Launch them. Put them into play. Remember, satisfied customers never refer you any business. By definition, they're just satisfied. It's the "wowed" customers that send you business. It's the wowed customers that will help you grow and that will become massive raving word of mouth maniac marketing promoters for you.

Do you need help to wow yours? Take the needed action. Build those power relationships. Stand out. Stay connected. Show them they're important and that you know them – better than anyone else. Build your brand better and purposefully.

Remember, don't be fooled or misled because these secrets may now seem simple or obvious, or perhaps "too easy." You understand how they could work for you now. Unleash your hidden weapons of mass promotion. Launch these 7 secrets. Do it and watch your income and your business explode!

About the Author

Larry Gassin is a peak-performance and success strategist with more than twenty years experience as a business and leadership coach advisor working with executives, entrepreneurs and high performance professionals.

As a C.P.A. he started his own firm and successfully competed against national and regional firms to win clients. While at the largest of the "Big 8" firms, he was selected as one of eleven members nationally to develop the firm's litigation consulting practice and was heavily involved in historic litigation matters including U.S. v. IBM and U.S. v. ABC, CBS Networks.

Larry also has in-depth entrepreneurial experience as the President and CEO of an energy systems technologies company he founded that has done business with resorts, major hotels, restaurants, major shopping malls, hospitals, apartment complexes, manufacturing facilities and homeowners across the nation. Specific clients have included Marriott, Embassy Suites and Doubletree hotels, South Coast Plaza shopping mall, Texaco/Shell, Penhall Diamond and Citadel National Management Company, among others.

He has written articles; been interviewed in magazines and on TV; addressed an international conference of world leaders on combating human trafficking and slavery; and spent 5 years as an ecclesiastic leader with a congregation of almost 500 while operating his businesses and along with his wife, raising their 4 children, who are among the most well-rounded and awesome people he knows.

Meet him and learn more about his speaking and training at: www.AdvancedCoachingSolutions.com and www.LarryGassin.com

www.ingramcontent.com/pod-product-compliance
Lightning Source LLC
Chambersburg PA
CBHW050513210326
41521CB00011B/2435